THE OAKWOOD PRESS

HUNSLET 1215

A War Veteran's Story

by
I.G. Hughes

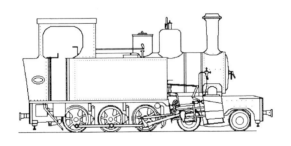

THE OAKWOOD PRESS

British Library Cataloguing in Publication Data
A Record for this book is available from the British Library
ISBN 978 0 85361 709 9

Typeset by Oakwood Graphics.
Repro by PKmediaworks, Cranborne, Dorset.
Printed by Cambrian Printers, Aberystwyth, Ceredigion.

The War Office Locomotive Society

Restoration, Remembrance, Recreation

The society had its origins in research into the history of the Hunslet War Office 4-6-0 locomotive which subsequently evolved into an online newsgroup. The formal offshoot of this developed when momentum built to try and locate an example of the type to repatriate, the subsequent story of which is told in this book.

Now that the War Office Locomotive Society has succeeded in its initial aim and, with the help of Locomotion and now the Moseley Railway Trust, have maintained the locomotive in publicly accessible, dry and secure locations, the next target is full sympathetic restoration to working order.

Although sometimes little appears to be happening on the surface the War Office Locomotive Society is working away behind the scenes exploring all avenues for funding that could see the project to completion. One step that has now been completed is the formation of the War Office Locomotive Trust which has also successfully applied for and been given charitable status (Charity No. 1136914). If, like us, you want to see a War Office Hunslet back in action then your support is vital so please contact the society either through Oakwood Press, or www.wols.org.uk

Published by The Oakwood Press (Usk), P.O. Box 13, Usk, Mon., NP15 1YS.
E-mail: sales@oakwoodpress.co.uk
Website: www.oakwoodpress.co.uk

Contents

No. 1215 derelict at Invicta Mill in 1965.   *Peter Neve*

Acknowledgements

The author would like to thank all those who have supplied information, photographs, and references which have gone into this work, without whose contributions this publication would not have been possible.

All photographs are by the author or courtesy of the individuals or organizations as marked, with apologies if any have been incorrectly identified. Any further information, photographs or corrections will be gratefully received.

It should be noted that many of the photographs are scans of old prints and as such may not be to present day photographic standards, however, the author is grateful that they do exist as they provide a pictorial record of 1215's history.

Introduction

Builder	Hunslet Engine Company of Leeds
Works No.	No. 1215 of 1916
Type	War Office
History	World War I

One of a class of locomotives built to the order of the British War Department for use by what became the Directorate of Light Railways. This organization used 600mm gauge railways to supply the trenches by bridging the gap between the end of the standard gauge railways and the relatively static front line of World War I on the Western front. They were used to move huge quantities of troops, casualties, shells, rations and other supplies over a network that, at its full extent, included over 3,000 miles of track.

What is significant about these locomotives?

Apart from being one of the largest classes of one single type of narrow gauge locomotive built within the UK, the vast majority were also completed within the space of three years. A total of 155 of them were ordered by the War Department from the Hunslet Engine Co. at a time when Hunslet were also constructing howitzers, shells, and machinery to make shells, as well as a limited number of other locomotives. By comparison, in peacetime they averaged about 40 locomotives of all types per year.

The other remarkable feature of these machines is the diverse locations in which they, and the nine built post-war, ended up. From hydro-electric schemes of the Scottish Highlands, to the pampas of Argentina, Harrogate gasworks to Australian canefields, Oxfordshire ironstone to Palestinian power stations, Nepalese forests and Chilean nitrate mines, all made good use of these neat little locomotives.

Chapter One

The Hunslets Get Call-Up Papers

Before the start of World War I, the British Military anticipated that the next major conflict would be a war of movement, where a mobile army could be supported by road transport. By contrast the Germans and French had more of a defensive mentality. Pre-war both of the latter countries had been building up fixed defensive positions and had also amassed large stocks of 600 mm gauge railway equipment.

Following the commencement of hostilities, by late 1914 it was apparent that the front lines had ground to a halt with both sides becoming entrenched. The more dug in they became, the more supplies were required to maintain the defences, and consequently an even greater amount of armaments and manpower were required to mount any kind of attack. For example, over the 153 days of the Somme offensive in 1916 almost 28 million shells were fired along a 14 mile front line, a little under 4,000 tons of high explosive every single day.

This put even more pressure on the supply lines. The main line railways could get no closer than four or five miles from the front, as they were a prime target for artillery, and were expensive to install and maintain. The primitive roads of compacted chalk collapsed with the rain and under the quantity of lorries and horses that were used, all of which tied up vast amounts of manpower in their operation and maintenance for the quantity of material that was moved.

Recognizing that logistics was becoming of immediate concern if the war was not to be lost, the War Office commissioned a report by Sir Eric Geddes, Deputy General Manager of the North Eastern Railway (NER) in early 1916. This report made a study of methods of moving war material to the front line, and noted that both the French and German war machines used 600 mm gauge equipment as a means of dealing with the distribution of supplies. On the ground, some of the British forces had already realised the benefit of light railways for themselves.

With the frequent reallocation of sections of front line between the Allies, and the occupation of areas captured from the Germans, the troops found sections of railway coming under their control and were quick to adopt them for their own benefit. Even if it was just a short hand-pushed trolley line from a store or nearby road to the trench or gun position, it could reduce manpower used and speed up deliveries.

The British High Command subsequently placed orders for a well designed and largely standardized set of light railway equipment. The track could be laid with minimal earthworks across broken ground, quickly and easily lifted, and re-laid if the front line moved, providing a reliable all-weather means of moving the vast tonnages required from the main line railhead up to the trenches themselves.

From October 1916, this material started to arrive in France, and made a positive difference in starting to turn the tide in the Allies favour. By 1917, an

Apart from supplies the railways proved an efficient way of moving vast numbers of troops to and from the front.

Imperial War Museum/Q2641

Packhorses near Thiepool in November 1916 on a road reduced to a morass by the heavy traffic. *Imperial War Museum/Q65389*

average of 165,530 tons of war material was being moved per week. A peak of 210,808 tons was reached in September 1917 in connection with the Battle of Ypres, and this was only material for the British sector of the front line. The French and the Americans each had similar systems for their own logistical supplies.

To provide motive power for this vast railway operation, the War Office ordered a total of 665 steam locomotives, 1,083 petrol locomotives and 12,960 wagons for the campaign in France. Further equipment was ordered for the fronts in Salonika, Italy, Egypt, Mesopotamia and Africa. Of the wagons, 5,099 were bogie wagons (early types B and C, plus later types D, E, F and H, with the latter being water tank wagons), 5,046 tipping wagons including Vee skips, and the remainder being miscellaneous such as the P class ration wagons.

Amongst the range of locomotives required, the specification for a larger steam locomotive for longer runs resulted in orders being placed with The Hunslet Engine Company of Leeds and Baldwin in America. The latter were used as Hunslet were unable to supply the quantity required quickly enough due to the limited capacity of its works and the large amount of other war work being undertaken.

By the Armistice in November 1918, these trench railways totalled over 3,700 miles of track in the British sector alone. The common gauge of 600 mm frequently allowed each side to commandeer enemy track and equipment as the front line moved, assisting in the aim of transporting personnel and supplies efficiently and effectively. The weight of rail used was mostly 20 lb. per yard (10 kg/m) of which there were 2,500 miles. However significant quantities of 16 lb. per yard (8 kg/m) were also used, as well as 9 lb. per yard (4.5 kg/m). These latter were unsuitable for locomotive traction and were used for lightly-laid hand-worked lines right up to the front line trenches.

Hans Sauer HE867 of 1905 supplied to the Lomaguada Railway Company, which served the Ayrshire gold mines in Southern Rhodesia.

Hunslet Engine Co.

Chapter Two

Specification and Construction

Part of the War Office specification was for the design to have a maximum axle loading of 4 tons. As Don Townsley describes in his history of the company, Hunslet were adept at continuously modifying and combining previous designs to meet requests for orders. A scan through the design catalogue found the 'Hans Sauer' class built for use in Southern Rhodesia (now Zimbabwe).

These were an 0-6-0T of roughly the correct proportions. With the design suitably adjusted by the addition of a bogie to reduce axle loading, and also give a better ride (but as later realised only in one direction), the 'War Office' type was born. The extra length also allowed the extension of the side tanks and the movement of the coal bunkers to behind the cab rather than short sections at the back end of each side tank.

This resulted in a locomotive capable of hauling 286 tons on level track, a maximum working axle loading of 3 tons 10 cwt, and able to work around 100 ft radius curves with ease.

The final design also included one or two features unusual for what was ostensibly a simple austerity design, one being rubber secondary suspension to protect the conventional springs from shocks on poor track. The second was the use of inside frames, unusual for Hunslet on so narrow a gauge, and was probably just a carry over from the 'Hans Sauer', but may have been to keep down the axle loading, as it removed the extra weight of axle extensions, fly-cranks and longer frame stretchers. A copper firebox and brass tubes were also retained, although a concession was made for the works and number plates which were from cast iron.

The first locomotive, Hunslet Works No. 1213, allocated War Office number 301, came off the production line on the 10th August, 1916 and was tried in steam a few days later. From the date of the order, through design to completion took a mere five months.

The next page is the equivalent of No. 1215's birth certificate. It is an extract from the Hunslet Engine Company's order book detailing order 37400 for the initial 10 locomotives. Although the entry was made and a Hunslet order raised on 22 March, details were still being confirmed in the last two weeks of May with the expected delivery of the first two to take place on 1st June, to be inspected by Messrs Rendell, Palmer & Tritton, consultant engineers to the War Office.

Note the reference to dull black for the overall paintwork, though reference to the painting records show this was actually relieved by red-oxide inside the frames and khaki cab interior.

The Hunslet record book gives a steaming date for No. 1213 of 5th August, 1916 dispatched on 10th August, with No. 1215 being the second of its type to leave for the front, on 12th August. For whatever reason No. 1214 was held until the 16th August and departed alongside No. 1216.

Despite the factory being tied up with other essential war work, Hunslet managed to produce 37 of the locomotives in 1916, 38 in 1917, and 33 in 1918.

178.

MARCH   37402.

22nd.   H.E.Co.Ltd

1916 ✓.

       50 Traversing Blocks Item P on drg 36958 /20694.

               37400.   *91/?*

War Office,Whitehall,London S/W/

10 Locomotives for 60 cm.(1'-11$\frac{5}{8}$") gauge of Railway

✓.   Type 4-6-0 Side Tanks with outs cyls 9½" x 12"

Design to T.N.12722

       Makers Nos. *1213 to 1222.*

May 20 — Engines to be painted Dull Black.

       1 Set of Hand Made Tracings to Inspector Spec. 4/1915 Clause 8

       Estimate: Page 30-File No.8

       Delivery: *2 by June 1st. 1916 & complete by 31st October 1916.*

       Inspection: *Messrs. Rendel Palmer & Tritton.*

       Marking letters. – W$_A$II.

                37403.

22 –   W.Scott & Middleton Ltd

         Contractor's Office,Pembrey,

         Burry Port,Carmarthenshire.

✓.   4 Buffer springs "A" pattern (off stock)

                For Loco No.257 (Lord Colville)

Delivery: To Pembrey G.W.R

       Re- 37400.   *Priority 2.*

                      S. No. 2000 to 2044

For full particulars of –   *M/M. 14 Oct- 191.*

1. Consignment- instructions.

2. Marking of Packages.

3 & 4. Copies of advice Notes.

           See Rendel. Palmer & Trittons letter

                   of May 31. 1916.

Extract from the Hunslet order book.

THE HUNSLET ENGINE CO. LTD *Engineers* LEEDS ENGLAND

4-6-0 TYPE

SIDE TANK ENGINE

Gauge of Railway	1 ft. 11½ in. (60 cm.)
Size of Cylinders	9½ in. dia. × 12 in. stroke
Dia. of Coupled Wheels	2 ft. 0 in.
,, Bogie Wheels	1 ,, 6½ ,,
Rigid Wheelbase (Engine)	5 ,, 6 ,,
Total Wheelbase (Engine)	13 ,, 0 ,,
Height from Rail to Top of Chimney	8 ,, 11½ ,,
Extreme Width	6 ,, 3½ ,,
Heating Surface—Small Tubes ... ... 168 sq. ft.	
,, ,, Firebox ... ... 37 ,,	
Total ... ... 205 ,, ...	205 sq. ft.
Grate Area	3·95 ,,
Working Pressure	160 lbs. per sq. in.
Tank Capacity	375 gallons
Fuel Space (Coal)	15 cwts.
Weight Empty (Engine)	10 tons 18 cwts.
,, in Working Order (Engine)	14 ,, 1 ,,
Total Weight on Coupled Wheels	10 ,, 10 ,,
Maximum Axle Load	3 ,, 10 ,,
Tractive Effort at 75 per cent. of Boiler Pressure	5415 lbs.
Ratio Adhesive Weight ÷ Tractive Effort	4·34
Minimum Radius of Curve Engine will traverse with ease	100 ft.
Weight per Yard of Lightest Rail advisable	20 lbs.
Load Engine will haul on Level	286 tons
,, ,, ,, up Incline of 1 in 100	143 ,,
,, ,, ,, ,, ,, 1 in 50	80 ,,

*Code Word—***WAROF**

C P 12 400—2/32

Order **37400**

ORDER Nº **37400**

Hunslet Engine Co.

General Arrangement drawing.

They then quietly completed the contract during 1919, turning out the remaining 47, although the War Office requested the last 20 be turned out to 2 ft 6 in. gauge. This was a popular gauge with many of the colonial railways so obviously they hoped it would help in finding a market for the now surplus locomotives.

War Office Order No.	Hunslet Order No.	Hunslet Works No.	War Office No.	Comments
DRT 648	37400	1213-1222	301-310	Initial order
DRT 648	37460	1223-1257	311-345	Extended by 35 locos
DRT 891	37930	1258-1287	346-375	
Egrail 1381	38810	1295-1334	2323-2362	
REQ.1839	39170	1336-1375	3220-3259	

As supplied they carried two re-railing jacks on the front footplate (even painted with the locomotives Light Railway Operating Directorate (LROD) number), and although not evident on any photographs there were also studs on top of one of the tanks to secure re-railing ramps too.

Bearing in mind that much of the skilled manpower had volunteered or been called up for military service and women had been hurriedly trained to keep the work going, this was a quite remarkable effort by the Hunslet Engine Company. However, it was not fast enough for the immediate demands of the War Office. They found that with all other possible suppliers in the UK already heavily tied up with war work and a depleted workforce it was necessary to turn to the Americans. Baldwin of Philadelphia had an existing design of similar proportions which fitted the specification with little modification so they received an order for 495 which they promptly completed within seven months, an indication of the size of their factory as well as their mass construction methods.

Page 11 shows the standard format Hunslet locomotive specification sheet, which they used as sales material for all their locomotives. A series of works photographs of 304 were taken, with the side elevation used as shown. Note the telegram shorthand type name of 'Waroff'.

As was to be expected with a class built over three years there were a number of subtle and not so subtle variations over time. Those known about include:

- The substitution of rail sections for rolled steel joists for the derailment crash bars under each buffer beam.
- The fitting of flangeless centre driving wheels.
- The fitting of a water lifter, with a suction pipe stowed on the back of the cab.
- A trial of condensing apparatus on No. 1287, an experiment intended to allow the steam locomotives to venture closer to the front line without the tell-tale plume of steam, which could attract unwelcome enemy attention. Although apparently successful its use was rendered unnecessary by the success of the petrol-engined Motor Rail tractors, and No. 1287 (WO 375) was subsequently returned to the standard arrangement.
- The installation of auxiliary steam valves on the front of the dome, as also visible on No. 1287. This could be used to power lineside water pumps or other auxiliary equipment.
- A trial of oil firing.
- The last 20 were built to 2 ft 6 in. gauge as noted, although this was more to encourage sales than from a specific military requirement.

War Department Light Railway (WDLR) 375 HE1287 of 1917 with condensing gear.

Hunslet Engine Co.

Chapter Three

War Work

The Hunslet locomotives appear to have been quite popular in use, and apparently were preferred over the similar Baldwins. Possibly the narrower overall width with lower-mounted side tanks resulted in a more stable locomotive (the centre of gravity was 1½ inches lower and overall width was 9 inches narrower), particularly with the inside frames that both designs had. It is believed that units that had Hunslets tended to try and keep hold of them! Although there are a number of stills photographs available of the Hunslet locomotives in service, principally from the Imperial War Museum archive, no cine footage had come to light until recently. The newly available National Film Board of Canada archive has finally revealed film of the Hunslets in operation. Unfortunately the running numbers are illegible in many of these images, either still or moving.

Most of the class appear to have survived the war although around 20 have no further record after dispatch from Hunslet. It is possible some may have been dispatched to the front purely as a set of spares. This is unlikely, as surely if faced with a choice between a ready-to-roll complete new steam locomotive or another that was already worn and possibly damaged, logic would suggest the use of the new one and leave the old for spares. That said there may be a scenario where officialdom and procedure dictated that it was easier to release parts rather than a complete locomotive.

It is also highly likely that some were destroyed during the hostilities. One photograph shows an unidentified Hunslet between two Baldwins, one of which has been blown onto its side. Others may have been deliberately damaged by the Allied forces during successful German offensives, when it was not possible to withdraw the locomotives any further than the end of the operational railway.

In operation it appears that generally the larger locomotives such as the Hunslets worked trains made up to six or seven bogie wagons. This would give a trailing load of perhaps 70 to 80 tons if loaded with heavy gun ammunition. There are photogrpahs of quite lengthy trains in use when handling less dense loadings (e.g. personnel, fodder or trenching materials).

Hunslet 1215 in active service

The first order placed by the War Office with Hunslet was indent number DRT 648 of May 1916, allocated Hunslet Order No. 37400. This asked for 10 locomotives of which No. 1215 was numerically the third, but was actually the second locomotive dispatched, on 12th August, 1916 to service in France, allocated number 303 by the War Office.

W.J.K. Davies' work (*Light Railways of the First World War*) suggests that the earliest lines worked by Hunslets were in the area of Trones Wood towards gun

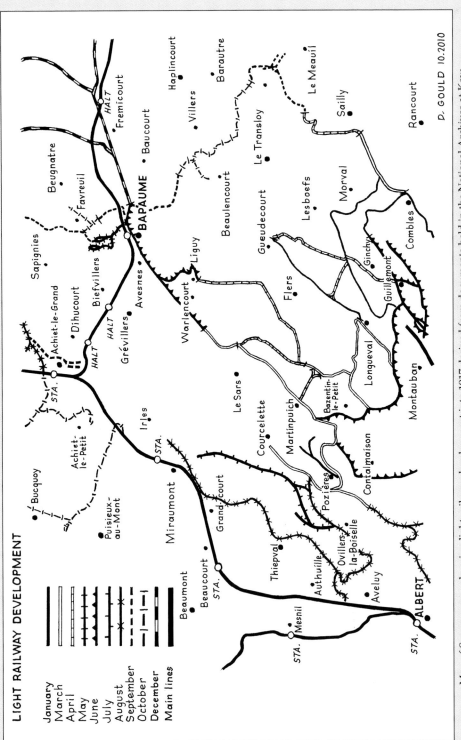

Map of Somme area, showing light railway development into 1917 derived from documents held in the National Archives at Kew.

D. GOULD 10.2010

LIGHT RAILWAY DEVELOPMENT

January
March
April
May
June
July
August
September
October
December
Main lines

WDLR309 HE1221 of 1916 and a variety of containers being watered simultaneously; note the icicles.

Imperial War Museum/Q1692

What looks like an attempt to damage or destroy a number of locomotives by derailing into a large shellhole, including Kerr, Stuart 202, Dick, Kerr 1983, four Hunslets (including 348 and 350) and two Baldwins, possibly near Pozieres. *BundesArchiv, Bild 104-0999G*

positions near Guillemont and Ginchy which were being constructed towards the end of the 1916 Somme offensive.

However the only confirmed record presently available of No. 1215's work behind the trenches is the well known photograph of it being serviced by American troops (*overleaf*). This is dated as September 1917 at Boisleux-au-Mont. A close look shows the effect of a year's war service; dents in the dome and a broken spectacle glass suggest that No. 1215 has been a bit closer to the action than this peaceful scene suggests.

After a little over two years of war service for No. 1215, hostilities ceased in November 1918. As with the soldiers themselves there was a progressive demobilization as equipment was cleared from different areas of the front. Salvage work carried on for some time with many locomotives and rolling stock gathered into large yards in preparation for a decision on their fate.

Some were sold directly from France whereas many were shipped back to the UK and stored, initially at the large military dock at Purfleet. Here they rubbed shoulders with some of the brand new Hunslets that were still under construction for another year after the war ended. Disposal of all now surplus military equipment was in the hands of the War Stores Disposal Board (WSDB).

Post-War Sales

Unlike the similar Baldwin-built locomotives there appears to have been much less difficulty in selling the Hunslets post-war, to the extent that Hunslet eventually built a further nine locomotives after the completion of the original War Office orders. It is, however, open to some speculation as to how much of these locomotives was actually new, as there are quite a few of the original production run that have no known post-war record.

The fact that the Hunslet locomotives were sought-after suggests that they would have commanded a higher price than the Baldwins. This was almost certainly a factor in the preference for the Baldwin locomotives by a certain light railway engineer and manager by the name of Colonel Holman F. Stephens. Brymbo Steel Works paid £1,500 for a used Hunslet for use at their ironstone quarries at Hook Norton (the unused locomotives were £275 more), whereas the Ashover Light Railway in Derbyshire bought their first four Baldwins for £1,000 each, and the last two for only £300 each.

As noted earlier, they ended up in extremely diverse locations, involving at least 17 different countries on all continents covering a range of duties in construction, agriculture, mining and public service operations. In general terms they appear to have met most success on railways with a decent length haul and moderate loads, rather than some the heavier work required on short steep mineral lines in the UK such as at Harrogate gasworks or Fauld gypsum mines.

Those that stayed in the UK were dispersed as follows:

This photograph is particularly significant in that of the surviving Hunslets around the world, No. 1215 is the only one that has a photograph of it in War Department Light Railway service in France during the war. Other photographs show Hunslets in various areas for example Hersin, which Davies suggests was the location of one of the first sections of official railway taken over by the British from the French, and which prompted the requirement for 'mainline' locomotives. As yet no records giving more detail of 1215's movements and allocations have been located but research will continue.

Imperial War Museum/Q6075

Operation/Location	Use	Locomotive Nos.
Stokes Bay	Military defences	1354 (until 1921), 1355 (until 1934)
Longmoor	Military training camp	1355 (from 1934)
Lochaber Railway, Fort William (Balfour Beatty then to J.N.Connell of Coatbridge for disposal)	Hydro scheme construction	1217, 1237, 1253 (until 1940), 1256, 1276 (until 1947), 1287
Churchill Barriers, Orkney	Defence construction	1253 (from 1940)
Fauld Mine, Tutbury	Mineral railway	1276 (from 1947)
Harrogate Gasworks	Mineral railway	1340
Hook Norton (Brymbo) Ironstone Quarry	Mineral railway	1264
Sydenham (Alfred Hickman) Ironstone Quarry	Mineral Railway	1324
Hartshill (Jees) Setts/Aggregate Quarry	Mineral Railway	1356
Avonmouth Lead/Zinc Smelter		1246
Hunslet Engine Co.	Parts, or rebuild for sale	1258, 1354 (from 1921)
George Cohen & Son	Equipment dealers	1268
Trevor Setts/ Aggregate Quarry	Mineral railway	1323

It is significant that none of the locomotives were sold to public service railways in various parts of the UK. Two possible reasons for this can be put forward. The first is that they may have been too small in size for the larger railways such as the Leek & Manifold or Lynton & Barnstaple. Secondly, Colonel Stephens, who was notoriously careful with money (rightly so in some cases), was directly or indirectly involved with most of the rest, and probably felt the £500 difference in price compared to the Baldwins was better spent elsewhere.

Hunslet, Alco-Cooke, Baldwin, Feldbahn, Barclay and Hudswell, Clarke locomotives being concentrated in a secure yard awaiting disposal.

Imperial War Museum/Q3668

Hunslet advertisement showing one of the more well-known British examples HE1340 of 1919, *Spencer*, cut down for Harrogate Gasworks after the war, as well as WDLR 304 HE1216 of 1916.

An early photograph at Bingera Sugar Mill; note extended smokebox, changed whistle and revised drawgear.

Ken Rogers Collection/Courtesy John Browning

Chapter Four

Demob and Army Surplus

Post-war No. 1215 was sold by the War Stores Disposal Board to the Engineering Supply Company of Australia (ESCA), possibly indirectly through Hunslet. Either way Hunslet had the job of preparing her and a number of other locomotives under order number 41755 for ESCA. It appears that the work required to regauge from 600 mm to 2 ft 0 in. was quite straightforward, the tyres were pressed out, replacement brake blocks and a rebuild plate fitted, before dispatch on 15th April, 1924.

The initial destination was the Bingera Sugar Mill of Gibson and Howes Ltd, located near Bundaberg north of Brisbane, Queensland Australia.

The east coast of Australia had an expanding sugar cane growing and processing industry, with the small sugar mills serving local farms. Narrow gauge railways, principally of 2 ft gauge played a significant part in the development of the industry, allowing much larger areas of cane to be accessible to the mills. This in turn led to an increase in the mills capacity to maximize efficiency (a process that still goes on today, with plantation areas being amalgamated to get improved mill efficiency with a highly modernized 2 ft gauge railway continuing to play a critical part).

No. 1215 worked at Bingera Mill, bringing sugar cane in for processing, until 1942. At this time a new boiler was fitted complete with extended smokebox, steel firebox (possibly due to wartime shortages) and a larger dome cover. This new boiler was built locally by the Bundaberg Foundry, and a copy of their drawing produced for this work was obtained during the initial stages of restoration in Australia. It is thought, however, that this boiler may not be entirely new as the steam pipes and regulator appear to have been transferred from the old boiler. Any other parts used will be identified once a copy of the original Hunslet boiler drawing can be obtained.

Following this reboilering, No. 1215 returned to work at Bingera Mill, continuing there until 1956. As the 1944 photograph shows, the Hunslet chimney was retained, as was the cab back plate and at least one of the WD 303 number plates. After 1956, Bingera sold No. 1215 to the Invicta Mill which is around 400 miles further up the coast near Townsville.

At Invicta Mill Hunslet 1226 (the eponymous *Invicta*) was out of use with a failed boiler, so No. 1215 was a good buy with a boiler only 14 years old. The mill then transferred the tanks, cab, name and spark arrestor off their locomotive onto the new arrival. No. 1215 also regained a set of original couplings to replace those fitted at Bingera.

The work required of locomotives on the cane railways is not to be underestimated, the intense harvest season needing a round-the-clock supply of cut cane to the mill to a schedule arranged between the different farms and the mill. This intense work was, and still is, completed using long rakes of unbraked loose-coupled wagons. The sizes of the wagons and locomotives have increased and the standard of permanent way has improved but problems such as described next also still occur.

At Bingera in October 1944, after the Bundaberg Foundry rebuild.

Also at Bingera in October 1944, at work alongside a Decauville 0-4-2T.

John Buckland/John Browning Collection

An early photograph of No. 1226 at Invicta Mill, the original jacks are still in place and the only visible modification is the spark arrestor.

John Browning Collection

The next photographs and notes illustrate 1215 at work at Invicta in October 1961 and were recorded and provided by John Knowles.

At the Haughton River just south of the mill there was a steep bank down to and back up from a low level bridge shared with the Bruce Highway, the major road up the east coast of Queensland. The grades necessitated splitting the loaded train at the top of the south bank and proceeding across the bridge and up the north bank in two sections.

However, all did not go to plan as part way up the bank a coupling parted and the tail end of the rake ran away back onto the bridge. The crew realised and whistled vigorously to warn any road traffic, then stowed the remaining portion at the top of the bank before returning to retrieve the runaways from the bridge where they had come to rest after rolling back and forth a few times.

After coupling they pulled the runaways up the bank, and stowed them before returning to collect the other half of the original rake. This was still of considerable length so was brought down briskly to make a run at the north bank, which was breasted at barely walking pace.

No. 1215 carried on working at Invicta Mill for another three years before withdrawal in 1964 following 40 years of work in Australia. Possibly No. 1215 was kept as a reserve locomotive, as it was a further three years before it started out on what came to be the long road home.

No. 1215 assembles a train of loaded cane trucks at a farm loading point to the south of the Haughton River. These will have been loaded in the fields on temporary track and pushed to the collection sidings by hand, horse, or tractor. *John Knowles*

A view of No. 1215 from October 1959 showing the modifications to the cab back plate, two of the water lifter hose brackets remain (these will be off No. 1226 as 1215 did not have them as built), and just visible above the left-hand cylinder is a mechanical lubricator, fitted since the 1944 photograph.   *Jim Longworth, John Browning Collection*

No. 1215 sets off across the fields with a lengthy loaded train for the mill.   *John Knowles*

Here No. 1215 crosses the bridge with the first section.   *John Knowles*

No. 1215 retrieving the runaways.   *John Knowles*

No. 1215 working up the bank with the second half of the rake.   *John Knowles*

Chapter Five

Retirement and the Long Journey Home

Retirement by the sea

In 1967 No. 1215 was presented to the Rowes Bay Children's Home in Townsville where it resided in a playground only 200 metres from the sea.

Twenty-eight years later No. 1215 was still there, the cycle of the years only broken by the occasional fresh coat of paint and some patching of the rotting side tanks. By this time the home had closed and the goverment department controlling Children's Homes had to decide what to do with this relic that they had inherited. Fortunately No. 1215 did not succumb to the fate of a number of other locomotives that were removed from parks in the late 1970s and early 1980s which were scrapped before their historical value was realised and preservationists could act.

After some debate, No. 1215 was sold by tender which as it turned out was not a straightforward process. At a public opening of tenders, the Service Club which had placed the locomotive in the park claimed possession. The goverment department responded by threatening to levy rental on the locomotive site for the duration of its residency. That cooled the Service Club's enthusiasm. Next, Townsville City Council entered the fray stating that the locomotive should stay in the city, however, the best offer from a Townsville resident was just a few hundred dollars. This offer was then rejected. Tenders from Victoria and New South Wales were over $30,000 dollars but, amongst other things, apparently failed to mention or acknowledge the heritage of the locomotive or guarantee its non-commercial future or to guarantee its restoration.

Alan Robert must have scored ticks in the right boxes and eventually secured the locomotive at a price less than the above figures. Of course like all these restorations, buying the locomotive was the cheapest part, the cost of transferring No. 1215 over 1,300 km by road to Brisbane was itself significant. Once in his workshop a start was made on stripping the locomotive and repairing the attrition caused by prolonged exposure to the sea air.

This progressed well, considering that Alan was working largely by himself, and also moved house, 1215 and his other projects twice during his ownership. Although superficially the locomotive looked reasonably tidy, dismantling revealed the extent of the damage caused by 28 years at the seaside. Rust pitting on the tyres was built up and turned, cab and tank drawings were obtained from Armley Mills Museum (with assistance from the author) to allow reconstruction of these items and an original Hunslet chimney was borrowed from the Australian Narrow Gauge Railway Historical Society at Woodford to use as a pattern for a new casting. However, by 2004 Alan's circumstances had changed and he felt it appropriate to let someone else have a go.

No. 1215 in the grounds of the Children's Home in Townsville   *Peter Neve*

No. 1215 after initial stripdown in Alan's workshop   *Author*

The long journey home

From about 1996 the now Chairman of the War Office Locomotive Society (WOLS) group had been in touch with the owner out of interest in the locomotive, and had never hidden the fact that he would like to see one back in the UK. In 2004 the owner gave him that opportunity, and with contacts previously made, a group was formed to take advantage of this offer. Australian cultural heritage rules dictate that a permit must be obtained before any heritage item may be removed from the country. So in compliance with this requirement an application was made which was subsequently rejected. It was, however, possible to appeal, which was done on the grounds that there were a further four locomotives remaining in Australia, all of which were on public display, and of these No. 1218 was in the Australian War Memorial in Canberra. Fortunately for us No. 1215 did not have anything in its history that made it stand out from the others. In addition, if it had been Australian troops doing the servicing in the photograph in 1917 (*page 20*) then there would probably have been no point in trying further. However, fortunately for WOLS the opinions of two of the expert examiners along with our contribution was sufficient to persuade the Federal Minister to approve our appeal which was granted before Christmas 2004, and by the following July the deal was done.

The other part of the story was the need to raise funds quietly. The reasons for this were two-fold, firstly to respect the privacy of Alan Robert, as many Australian enthusiasts would have preferred the locomotive to stay, and the second was to make sure the locomotive stayed with a group whose intention was to make sure that No. 1215 stayed on public display rather than be bought by an individual for a private collection. A prudent decision as it turned out as during the period while funds were being raised Alan was made a significant unsolicited offer, however, to his credit and to the gratitude of WOLS he stayed faithful to the original agreement.

After much drawing, discussion and planning, it was confirmed that No. 1215 would fit in a standard 20 ft shipping container, just! This required the removal of the upper cab, dome, chimney and couplings, with rails on the container floor made of hardwood strips to keep the height as low as possible. It all just fitted. With a length of timber across each buffer beam No. 1215 was the same length as the inside of the container so very unlikely to move.

The Hunslet was pushed into a container by Alan's immaculately restored Caterpillar D2, braced by the timbers on the buffer beams and attached to the container floor with ropes. The rest of the components were secured in the bunker, the cab or on the floor of the container and finally No. 1215 was ready to go. So with significant assistance from another Australian enthusiast and P&O shipping (now part of the Maersk group), the retired war veteran started on its way, back to the land of its construction.

After a brief pause in New Zealand, the Canadian Pacific container ship *Aurora* then headed straight for Tilbury via the Panama canal. Depending on No. 1215's original export route it may in fact have circumnavigated the world. After 81 years away from the United Kingdom, No. 1215 put her wheels on home rails at a private location in Hampshire on 23rd September, 2005.

A lesson in how to get a quart into a pint pot, the container is opened in September 2005.

Rob Bance

Various motion parts, and new chimney casting to top left.   *Author*

Chapter Six

Hunslet 1215 in the UK

When the container door seals were cut, and they creaked open it was the start of a whole new stage of No. 1215's life. As 1215 was extracted from the container it was partially reassembled, and it was great satisfaction to see a War Office Hunslet back on British soil.

While No. 1215 was dismantled, engineering assessments were sought for the boiler and the rest of the locomotive. These suggested that for a full professional restoration to working order the costs would be of the order of £250,000. The boiler is repairable. However, being of Belpaire design, and with a very narrow firebox, it would require complete dismantling to access the sections that needed repair so the costs will be close to that required for a new boiler. Although the locomotive was largely complete, it had had a very hard working life and everything was worn to a greater or lesser degree. The period by the seaside in Townsville had not done it any favours either. However, the frames were straight and almost unaffected by corrosion, the tyres were thick, and the previous owner had provided new tanks, bunker and new cast chimney.

The society made the decision that the locomotive should be largely reassembled and put in an appropriate condition for display until such time as sufficient funds were available to make a realistic start on restoration, rather than the parts being scattered and the locomotive disappearing from view while slow progress was made.

An idea of the number of components that go into a small steam locomotive is given by the following sequence of photographs. At a basic level, almost all steam locomotives contain the same set of components, albeit different sizes and designs, but they will all be there. Though when comparing restoration costs with the familiar 0-4-0ST 'Quarry' Hunslet, No. 1215 has five axles rather than two, resulting in 10 sets of axleboxes and springs rather than just four!

After reassembly and a coat of protective primer, No. 1215 headed north in March 2006, to accept an invitation for display at Locomotion, the National Railway Museum outstation museum at Shildon, with an outing to Hollycombe Steam Railway in July for a special event.

In February of the following year a further working party applied a coat of semi-gloss black, which although shiny at first has subsequently dulled down to the kind of finish we believe the War Office originally requested.

In early 2008, a rearrangement of National Collection items meant that No. 1215's space at Shildon was needed, at which stage discussions were held to identify an appropriate and secure site to which to move the locomotive. Agreement was made with the Moseley Railway Trust (MRT) to move to the Apedale Heritage Centre near Newcastle-under-Lyme where they are building a new railway. The MRT is also assembling an extensive collection of former WDLR equipment including examples of the different bogie wagons and Simplex locomotives, all of which provide the ideal complement to No. 1215.

Cab and backhead equipment, including steam brake valve, cylinder lubricators and at top right a water lifter and the pulley for carrying the cord for pulling the whistle!

Author

The move took place on 13th July, 2008 with No. 1215 being offloaded by MRT members, the first time the locomotive had stood on a full railway (as against an odd section of track) since leaving Invicta Mill in 1967.

At the very successful first MRT Apedale Valley Light Railway open day, 1215 was displayed in front of restored D and H class wagons as well as a Hudswell, Clarke 0-6-0WT. This locomotive was built in 1916 to the same design as those supplied by Hudswell, Clarke to the War Office. However, a more poignant moment came later in the year.

In November an event was held for Remembrance Sunday with half the profits from MRT and WOLS being donated to the British Legion and for the first time in 90 years No. 1215 came face to face with an old friend in the shape of a Protected Simplex LR3090, MotorRail 1369 of 1918.

The Simplex locomotives (or 'tractors' as they were known in the WDLR) worked hand-in-hand with the War Office Hunslets, typically covering areas right next to the front where they were less visible to enemy observation. In fact the success of these locomotives curtailed the development of the condensor for the steam locomotives as noted earlier, and laid the foundations to a design that was still being produced in the 1990s. LR3090, part of the MRT collection, was built just as the war finished and went immediately to Purfleet for sale into industrial use. It found work in the Knostrop sewage treatment works of Leeds Corporation until the 1960s when it was laid up with a gearbox problem. Restored in 2001 as part of the Salvage Squad TV series from Channel Four, it is now in full working order and runs from time-to-time for special events.

Injectors and other steam fittings.   *Author*

Author

Springs, axle box keeps, bogie side control springs and the secondary suspension rubbers..

Brake gear including a very worn brake column shaft at the front. *Author*

The evening of installation at Shildon, with some very illustrious company.

At Hollycombe gala posed with a World War I steam road wagon.

Author

No. 1215 assisted onto Moseley Railway Trust rails by a pair of 20/28 Simplexes.

Phil Robinson

No. 1215 in the storage shed at Apedale on the first open day.

Armoured Simplex and Hunslet, with a Hudswell, Clarke in the background, 11th August, 2008.

Author

Hunslet WDLR303 (1215) and Baldwin WDLR778 reminisce together at Stonehenge works on Leighton Buzzard Light Railway.   *Cliff Thomas*

In 2009 the Leighton Buzzard Narrow Gauge Railway (LBNGR) requested No. 1215 for a visit, even though it is largely unrestored, as they were having a Gala weekend to celebrate the centenary of their Barclay locomotive *Doll*. *Doll* had worked in Sydenham ironstone pits along with two sister Barclays and another ex-WDLR Hunslet. So on this occasion *Doll* was reunited with one of its siblings *Gertrude* and a War Office Hunslet. The LBNGR is also the home of the operational ex-WDLR Baldwin 778, so of course the opportunity was taken to park the two of them together.

In due course there are still many other historic meetings which can take place, with the Welsh Highland Heritage Railway's *Russell* (which was also at Hook Norton), or with *Harrogate* and *Barber* from the Harrogate gasworks system, and there will be others!

Order number 37400 painted on the inside of the bogie frame.   *Rob Bance*

Connecting rod big-end bearing with brazed repair.   *Author*

Chapter Seven

Archaeology on 1215

As with most steam locomotives built in the UK almost all of No. 1215's components were stamped with its Hunslet locomotive number 1215 and a WD arrow. In some locations the WDLR number 303 was also added. These give a useful guide to the originality of components and later replacements, and can reveal some extra information and questions about the history of the locomotive. During the dismantling and conservation work so far completed a number of parts from other Hunslets have been found.

So far the following have been positively identified:

1216	Front draw bar pin
1213	Front drawbar bracket
1224	Steam brake handle, steam brake body and base
1219	Rear bogie axle
1213	Window catch
1239	Window catch
1279	Window top pivot (and 1215) 2 off
1265	Window top pivot (and 1215)

These locomotives were as follows:

1213 is meant to have gone to Argentina, but there is no record of it there, although another part does survive on 1332 preserved in Buenos Aires.

1216 went to an estate railway in Argentina.

1219 was dispatched to Proserpine mill in Queensland and scrapped by 1961. Further parts (brake hangers) survive on 1229 preserved at Woodford in Queensland.

1224 is alleged to have gone to Australia, but again there are no Australian records that confirm this.

1239 was dispatched to North Eton Mill in Queensland. This locomotive has survived and is now preserved at the Ipswich Workshops Museum in Queensland.

1265 dispatched to construction of the Rutenberg power station in Palestine, this locomotive survives in Israel preserved with a diesel power unit.

1279 to Buenos Aires and Great Southern agricultural feeder railways in Argentina.

The parts from other Australian locomotives are likely to have been swapped during the course of its stay out there, though curiously none so far have had 1226's stamp. The others are most likely to have been swapped during its rebuild by Hunslet, though there remains a possibility that they occurred during wartime maintenance.

Although the major parts of No. 1215 had been shotblasted in Australia, the bogie frame and sand dome missed out. The sand dome has yet to be rubbed down but with a bit of care it might reveal the original paint scheme. Some careful cleaning of the bogie frame revealed an original painted order number on the front cross member (*see overleaf*).

As visible in the photograph of No. 1215 at Bingera Mill the Bundaberg Foundry boiler had a substantial flange in the middle which required a wider

A vision of the future? No. 1215 hauls an H class water tank through the snow towards Apedale Road. Reality, rearrangement of the contents of the Aurora North shed left No. 1215 and the tank wagon temporarily out on the main line, and the opportunity was too much to resist, (with the help of a biscuit tin and some smouldering rags).   *Moseley Railway Trust*

lower section to the dome casing. This boiler also had an extended smokebox. Although done from practical necessity, both of these items slightly spoil the look of the locomotive. The extended smokebox was a very common modification to the Australian locomotives. This was presumably to make them more suited to a higher ash content fuel, or to give capacity to minimise the need for a clean out during the working shift. On dismantling it appears that No. 1215 does retain its original regulator valve and pipework as the support brackets have been modified to suit.

The sheet metal parts transferred from No. 1226 with the rebuild at Invicta Mill suffered badly from exposure and corrosion while at the Children's Home to the extent that only the diamond stack base, the cab front and sides, and the fittings and edging from the tanks and bunker survived.

Other modifications of uncertain era include fitting of larger main crank pins, the attachment of plain bearing leading ends to the coupling rods (rather than the split type), cutting and welding of the middle of the connecting rods and many welded repairs to the split bearing end of the connecting rods. The rods also now being held on by caps and bolts on the end of the pins rather than collars and cotter pins.

All of the motion has been fitted with grease nipples too. Presumably in its last years it was on borrowed time because of the influx of diesels. All bearings are worn, particularly the big-ends of the con-rods where one side has actually worn through the back end so a piece of plain brass has been brazed on to the outside! This was very much a bush repair for a machine with a limited life expectancy.

What next for 1215?

Although No. 1215 has been made presentable for static display, the plan is for a full restoration to working order. As noted earlier, 1215 is largely complete, but all the moving parts are very worn and although the boiler is technically repairable, the money may well be better spent on a new one which would guarantee a longer lifespan.

To achieve this in as sympathetic manner as possible will require significant time and money. Any enquiries or offers of assistance should be directed to the author via the Oakwood Press, at www.wols.org.uk

Chapter Eight

Other Survivors

Including No. 1215, it is believed that 14 of the final total of 164 locomotives still survive. All are in various stages of preservation or storage.

Australia

1218 of 1916

Formerly of Gin Gin Mill, survived after being found by a traction engine enthusiast in a scrapyard. It was taken to the Melbourne area and was occasionally operated at low pressure on a short section of track, without any injectors. After a further change of hands, No. 1218 was bought by the Australian War Memorial in Canberra and restored for museum display. Although a significant amount of work was completed it remains on static display or in the reserve store.

1229/1240

No. 1229 worked at Cattle Creek Mill alongside No. 1245, eventually inheriting some spare parts from it. It was known to have suffered a bent chassis after a collision at a flat crossing with a Queensland Goverment Railways (QGR) train and was suspected to have received the spare chassis from No. 1226. However, recent investigation found evidence that the frames were actually from No. 1240, along with a variety of parts off other Australian Hunslets, including No. 1219 which had donated an axle to No. 1215. Acquired by the Australian Narrow Gauge Railway Museum Society it is now stored at their operating railway at Woodford, north of Brisbane. It has a leading bogie wheelset of unknown origin with spoked wheels.

1239

Worked all its Australian life at North Eton Mill and was retired to static display in the local war memorial park for many years. It was removed from display after the local association responsible for the park began to find the insurance and maintenance liabilities too onerous. After a period in storage back at the now closed mill it was acquired by the Workshops Railway Museum based in the former QGR workshops at Ipswich. Here it has been on static display, but some funding for restoration work has recently been made available.

1317

This worked at Proserpine Mill with No. 1219. Again it was displayed in a local park, this time looked after by the local Rotary club. It has now had some cosmetic restoration work and is on display under cover in the local museum.

Brazil

1312

One of four that were exported through Robert Hudson to the EF Palmares Osorio, a general carrier railway in the Rio Grande do Sul area of Brazil. It survives somewhat gaudily painted along with one of the railway's coaches in a park.

1313

Has one of the more unusual survival stories. Before dispatch to Brazil it was rebuilt to metre gauge with an enlarged bunker and firebox for use at Usina Leao Utinga, a sugar mill in Alegoas State. Here it remained in obscurity to UK enthusiasts, until on a visit someone observed that an 0-6-2T had a number of Hunslet features, but there was no record of such a locomotive going there, just the 4-6-0T. Further investigation showed that the locomotive's frame had in fact been reversed, with the connecting rods now driving the rearmost set of driving wheels rather than the leading set. After a period with undergrowth growing up around it, the locomotive has now been cosmetically cleaned up and is believed to be still on display at the sugar mill.

Argentina

1332

Was supplied to the Buenos Aires and Great Southern Railway to operate the extensive agricultural feeder railway based on Balcarce. As demand moved to alternative transport it was transferred to bolster the motive power of the Corrientes Railway (also known as the Ferrocarril General Urquiza), a general carrier railway in Corrientes Province. Along with many of the other War Office Hunslet locomotives that ended up in Argentina the side tanks were removed and it ran with a bogie wagon converted to a tender. It is presently on static display outside the national railway museum in Buenos Aires.

1336

Almost identical in history to No. 1332, it is now preserved at the Estado Santa Anna, in Corrientes province.

1337

Again history as per No. 1332, it is now preserved at Estado Concordia in Entre Rios province.

Nepal

1536 and 1537

Rejoicing in the names *Guhyeshwari* and *Pashupati* this pair were built in 1926 to the order of the Nepal Government Railways, to 2 ft 6 in. gauge with a larger firebox and extended side tanks (in a similar style to *Russell* of the Welsh Highland Railway). They worked all their lives on the Jaynagar-Janakpur line near the Indian border. No. 1536 was noted dismantled in the early 1980s, however, remarkably, a new set of wheels was supplied by Hunslet and this locomotive was photographed in operation in 1994! As such it was the last of the class to remain in steam. The line is still open, and the steam stock remains in store with one of the larger 0-6-2T locomotives believed nominally available to support the diesels used.

India

1371

One of the post-war batch built to 2 ft 6 in. gauge has an unknown history between being supplied to India through Robert Hudson, and being found on static display in a private museum in an army camp near Pune. There was believed to have latterly been a railway for the amusement of staff families in use in the camp.

Israel

1265

Is known to have been used on post-war reconstruction work in France before being rebuilt and supplied for the construction of the Rutenberg hydro-electric power station on the River Jordan in what was then Palestine. It is believed that the locomotive was partially dismantled at the time of completion of the construction work. The power station was later destroyed in the turmoil from which the Israeli state emerged, and due to its location on the border the area was mined. Some years later a resident of a nearby kibbutz negotiated successfully to retrieve the remains, which included the largely complete chassis, with the tanks and cab separate, but no boiler. The locomotive has now been restored and reassembled, albeit with a diesel power unit in the boiler space and a mock-up boiler, and is now occasionally run with some skip wagons.

Bibliography

Light Railways of the First World War, by W.J.K. Davies, David & Charles.

Two Foot Gauge Rails to the Ironstone, by Paul Ingham, RCL Publications, ISBN 0 9538763 0 6.

Narrow Gauge at War, by Keith Taylorson, Plateway Press, ISBN 0 9511108 1 0.

Narrow Gauge at War 2, by Keith Taylorson, Plateway Press, ISBN 1 871980 29 1.

The Light Tracks from Arras, by T.R. Heritage, Plateway Press, ISBN 1 871980 40 2.

'Harrogate Gas Works', by Martin P.F. Hallows and David H. Smith, Narrow Gauge Railway Society, ISBN 0 9507169 6 0, ISSN 0142 5587 (Issue No. 146 of The *Narrow Gauge* from the NGRS).

'The Lochaber Narrow Gauge Railway', by Patrick Howat, Narrow Gauge Railway Society, ISBN 0 9507169 0 1, ISSN 0142 5587 (Issue No. 87/88 of *The Narrow Gauge* from The NGRS).

The Narrow Gauge No. 164 from the NGRS ISSN 0142-5587.

The Narrow Gauge No. 98 from the NGRS ISSN 0142-5587.

Narrow Gauge Railways in North Caernarvonshire, Vol. 1 The West, by J.I.C. Boyd, Oakwood Press, ISBN 0 85361 273 0.

Ironstone Quarries of the Midlands Part 2: The Oxfordshire Field, by Eric Tonks, Runpast Publishing, ISBN 1 870754 02 6.

The Hunslet Engine Works, by Don H. Townsley, Plateway Press, ISBN 1 871980 38 0

Model Railways April 1976.

Locomotives International No. 19, Paul Catchpole Ltd, ISSN 13537091 09.

Locomotives International No. 52 (Jan-Feb 2000), Paul Catchpole Ltd, ISSN 13537091 09.

Locomotives International No. 55 (Sept-Oct 2000) , Paul Catchpole Ltd, ISSN 13537091 09.

Industrial Railway Record No. 152 (March 1998) from the Industrial Railway Society.

'Los Paperos', *Ferroclub No. 29*, Ferroclub Argentino.

Hunslet Narrow Gauge Locomotives, by Andrew Neale, Plateway Press, ISBN 1 871980 28 3.